Miraculous Magic Tricks

MAGICAL ILLUSIONS

by Thomas Canavan

Illustrations by David Mostyn

WINDMILL
BOOKS

New York

Published in 2014 by Windmill Books, an Imprint of Rosen Publishing
29 East 21st Street, New York, NY 10010

First Edition

Author: Thomas Canavan
Editors: Patience Coster and Joe Harris
US Editor: Joshua Shadowens
Illustrations: David Mostyn
Design: Emma Randall

Library of Congress Cataloging-in-Publication Data

Canavan, Thomas, 1956–
  Magical illusions / by Thomas Canavan.
     pages cm. — (Miraculous magic tricks)
  Includes index.
  ISBN 978-1-4777-9049-6 (library) — ISBN 978-1-4777-9050-2 (pbk.) —
  ISBN 978-1-4777-9051-9 (6-pack)
  1. Magic tricks—Juvenile literature. I. Title.
  GV1548.C22 2014
  793.8—dc23
                        2013021322

Printed in the USA

CPSIA Compliance Information: Batch #BW14WM: For further information contact Windmill Books, New York, New York at 1-866-478-0556

SL003847US

CONTENTS

Introduction 4

The Magician's Pledge 5

Spoon Bend 6

Ping-Pong Palm 8

The Plastic Wand 11

Disappearing Straw 15

The Restored Napkin 17

Floating Water 20

Saw the Lady in Half 22

Where's the Orange? 26

Elastic Band Up the Nose 29

Further Reading, Websites,
Glossary, and Index 32

INTRODUCTION

Within these pages you will discover great magic tricks that are easy to do and impressive to watch.

To be a successful magician, you will need to practice the tricks in private before you perform them in front of an audience. An excellent way to practice is in front of a mirror, since you can watch the magic happen before your own eyes.

When performing, you must speak clearly, slowly, and loudly enough for everyone to hear. But never tell the audience what's going to happen.

Remember to "watch your angles." This means being careful about where your spectators are standing or sitting when you are performing. The best place is directly in front of you.

Never tell the secret of how the trick is done. If someone asks, just say: "It's magic!"

THE MAGICIAN'S PLEDGE

I promise not to reveal the secrets of magic to those who are not magicians.

I promise to practice these magic tricks **over** and over again before attempting to perform them in front of an audience.

I promise to respect my art, the art of magic.

SPOON BEND

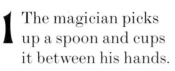

1 The magician picks up a spoon and cups it between his hands.

2 He holds the spoon so that his interlocking fingers hide the handle. The bowl of the spoon should jut out between his left and right little fingers.

3 He says that he will bend the spoon using his magical powers. He presses the bowl of the spoon against the table.

4 The magician pulls a face to make it look as though he is concentrating hard. He begins to loosen the grip of his fingers.

5 The bowl of the spoon moves forward. At the same time (and hidden from the spectators), the spoon handle swings across the palms of the magician's cupped hands. This sleight of hand makes it look as though the spoon has bent.

6 The magician quickly unlocks his fingers, picks up the spoon and shows it to the spectators to prove that it's back to normal.

PING-PONG PALM

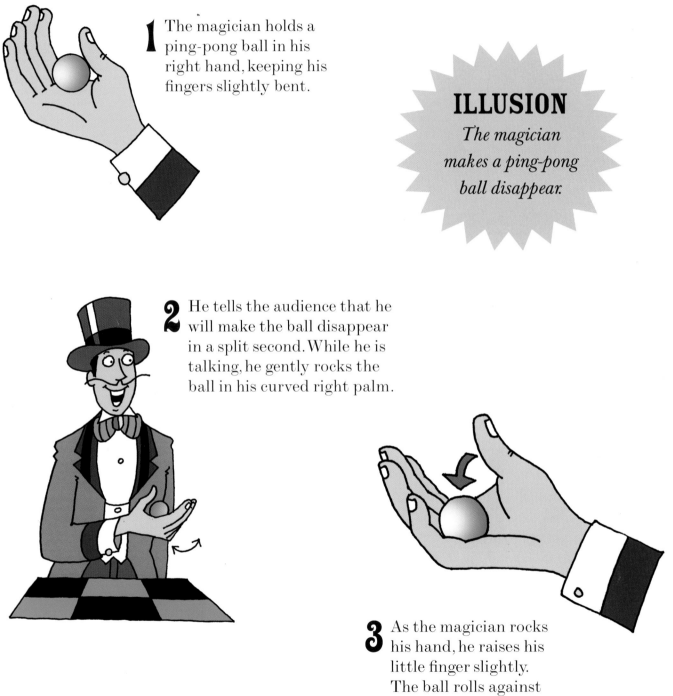

1 The magician holds a ping-pong ball in his right hand, keeping his fingers slightly bent.

ILLUSION

The magician makes a ping-pong ball disappear.

2 He tells the audience that he will make the ball disappear in a split second. While he is talking, he gently rocks the ball in his curved right palm.

3 As the magician rocks his hand, he raises his little finger slightly. The ball rolls against his little finger and stops.

4 The magician holds out his left hand, also slightly cupped, with the palm facing upward.

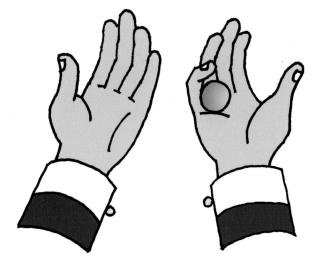

5 While the audience is distracted by the left hand, the magician curls his third and fourth right fingers over a little more. The ball now rests between these two fingers.

6 In one motion, the magician tightens his third and fourth fingers (holding the ball in place) and flips his right hand so that the palm is facing downward.

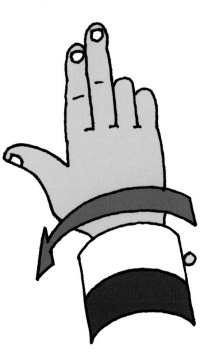

7 He passes his right hand over his cupped left hand. It looks as though the ball is dropping into his left hand.

8 The magician closes his left hand before his right hand has passed completely over it.

9 He moves his right hand down to his side and concentrates on holding his cupped left hand out. Then he slowly opens it to reveal—no ball!

NOT THERE

THE PLASTIC WAND

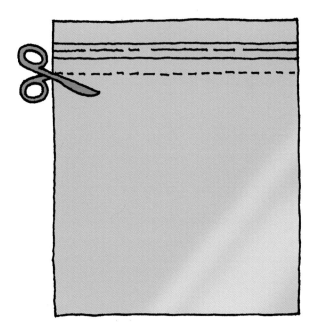

ILLUSION

The magician uses a "magic" hair from a member of the audience to guide a plastic wand back and forth.

1 Prior to the trick, the magician slices the end off a ziplock sandwich bag. He leaves about as much plastic below the zip as there is above it.

2 He snips a small strip off one end of this piece of plastic. The bit he snips should be narrower than his little finger.

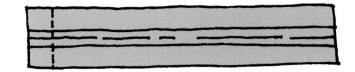

11

3 He secretly asks one of the spectators to be in on the trick later on.

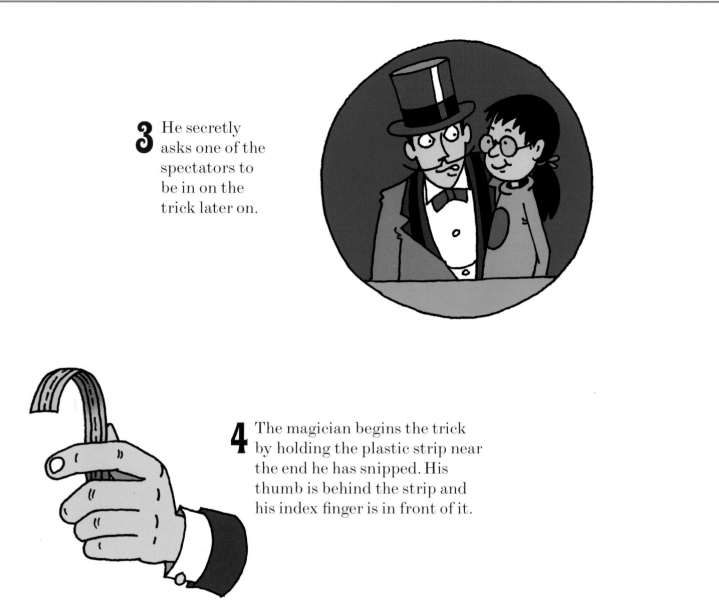

4 The magician begins the trick by holding the plastic strip near the end he has snipped. His thumb is behind the strip and his index finger is in front of it.

5 He tells the spectators that this is his plastic wand, even though it is flopping forward and looks nothing like a magician's wand.

6 The magician asks the spectators whether anyone has magic hair. He looks around and chooses his partner from the audience.

OUCH!

7 The magician's partner comes up and stands next to him. (The magician is still holding the wand in his hand.) The magician says, "Ah yes, definitely magic hair ..." and pretends to pluck a hair from his partner's head.

8 The magician holds the "hair" over the end of the wand. He pretends to wrap it around the wand a few times.

9 As he does this, he slowly drags his thumb along the wand. The end of the wand seems to be pulled back by the magic hair. The magician waves his other hand (with the magic hair) over the wand. He moves his thumb up the wand so that it seems to be pulled forward by the hair.

10 Finally, the magician pulls the magic hair (and wand) back and "drops" the magic hair. He slides his thumb quickly up the wand so that it flops forward.

DISAPPEARING STRAW

1 The magician holds a short length of drinking straw (about as long as his little finger) in his right hand, between the tip of his thumb and the tip of his middle finger. A little bit of the straw extends below his finger.

ILLUSION
The magician taps a piece of drinking straw into his right hand. But when he opens his hand, the straw has disappeared!

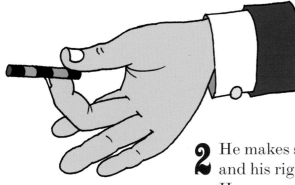

2 He makes sure that the straw is pointing straight up and his right palm is facing away from the audience. He announces that he will make the straw disappear.

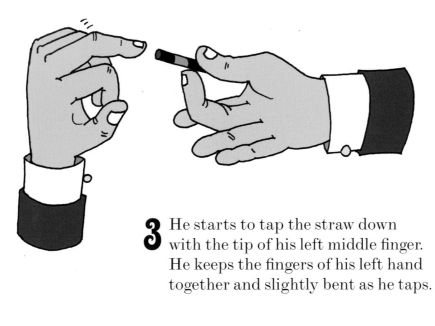

3 He starts to tap the straw down with the tip of his left middle finger. He keeps the fingers of his left hand together and slightly bent as he taps.

15

4 When the straw is almost tapped down, the magician taps the straw forward a little. The straw swings and the end of it hits the magician's left palm.

5 The magician secretly presses the straw into his left hand. (His left "tapping finger" presses it harder into his palm.) At the same time he clenches his right fist to make it look as though he's holding the straw there.

6 He moves his left hand (holding the straw) away and holds out his right fist. Then, with a flourish, he opens it to reveal—no straw!

THE RESTORED NAPKIN

1 The magician needs two paper napkins to make this trick work. He scrunches one of them into a tight ball and keeps it hidden in his slightly closed right hand.

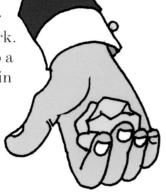

ILLUSION

The magician tears up a paper napkin, but at the end of the trick the napkin is revealed in one piece!

2 He puts a pencil into his back right-hand trouser pocket.

3 To start the trick, the magician tells the spectators he is going to tear a napkin and then restore it with his wand. He holds up a paper napkin and unfolds it. (He is still holding the scrunched-up napkin in his right hand.) He holds the napkin, stretched open, by the corners.

4 The magician tears the open napkin in half. He puts the pieces on top of each other and tears again. Now he has four pieces. The magician shows the spectators the pieces and then does another tear— now he has eight pieces.

5 He scrunches all of these pieces into a tight little ball (like the hidden ball) and closes his right hand over it. The other ball is sitting next to it, still hidden.

6 The magician says, "Now it's time to do some magic. Where's my wand?" In sight of the audience, he passes the un-torn napkin ball from his closed right hand and holds it up with his left hand. He waves this ball in his left hand to distract the spectators. The ball made of torn pieces is still hidden in his right hand.

7 With his right hand, he quickly stuffs the torn-up napkin ball into his back pocket and pulls out the pencil. He waves the pencil-wand over his left hand several times, then puts the wand down.

8 He slowly begins to unravel the ball in his left hand to reveal—a complete napkin!

FLOATING WATER

1 The magician shows the spectators a normal juice glass (made of glass, not plastic). He fills it to the brim with water.

2 He shows the audience a piece of thin card. He says he will give the card the magical power to hold the water in the glass— even when it's upside down.

3 He holds the glass in one hand and the card in the other and turns his back to the spectators.

4 The magician places the card on the rim of the glass, making sure it covers the glass completely. He continues to hold the glass with one hand and presses the card down on the rim.

5 Next the magician turns to the spectators again. He turns the glass upside down while holding the card tight against the rim.

6 The magician speaks to the card: "Now it's time to do your magic. Keep that water inside the glass." He takes his hand away and the card stays in place—no water comes out of the glass!

SAW THE LADY IN HALF

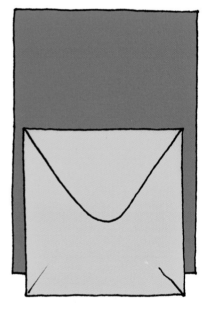

ILLUSION

The magician cuts a paper "lady" in half, but she emerges unharmed in this home version of the famous magic trick.

1 Prior to the trick, the magician gets an empty envelope (from a medium-sized birthday card) and a blank piece of paper. The envelope must be narrower than the paper.

2 The magician seals the envelope and snips off the sides. The envelope can now be opened into a tube.

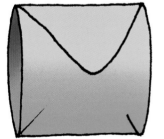

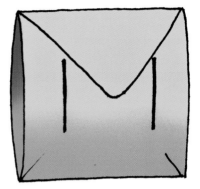

3 The magician cuts two slits across the back of the envelope, about a third of the way from each end.

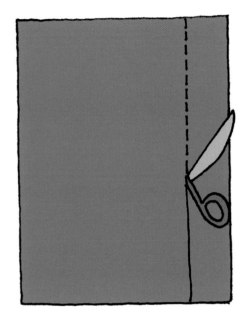

4 He cuts a strip from the longest side of the piece of paper. The strip should be a little narrower than the slits on the envelope.

5 The magician draws a picture of a lady on this strip. She can be just a stick figure, but she should extend the whole length of the strip, with her head near one end and her feet at the other.

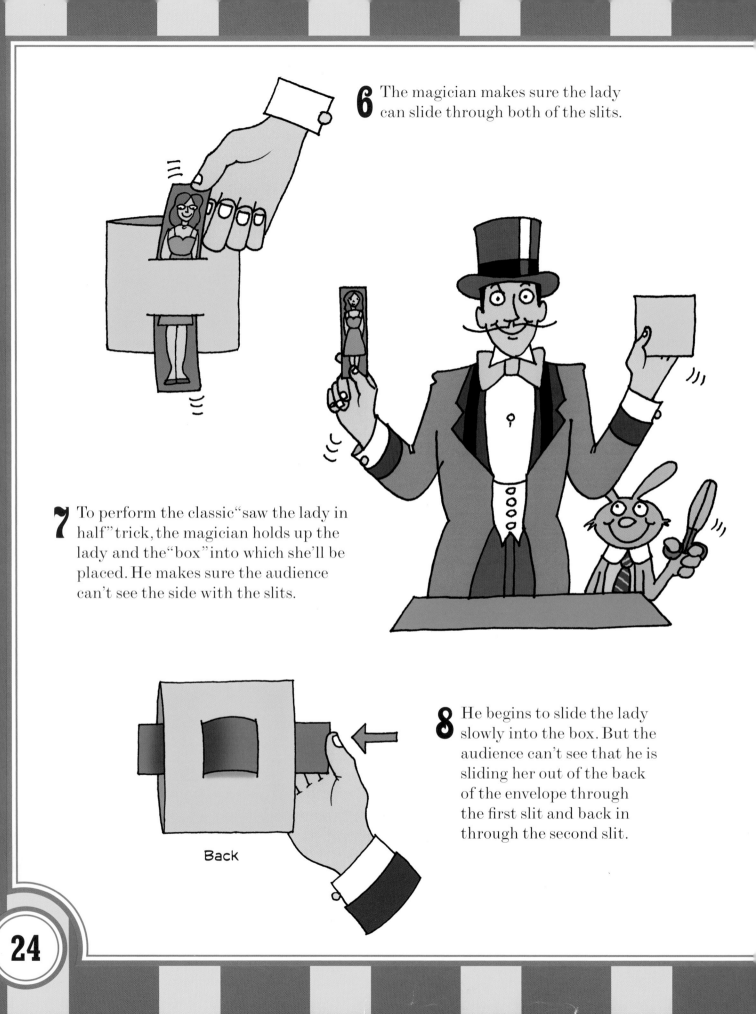

6 The magician makes sure the lady can slide through both of the slits.

7 To perform the classic "saw the lady in half" trick, the magician holds up the lady and the "box" into which she'll be placed. He makes sure the audience can't see the side with the slits.

Back

8 He begins to slide the lady slowly into the box. But the audience can't see that he is sliding her out of the back of the envelope through the first slit and back in through the second slit.

9 With the lady sticking out of each end of the box, the magician lays the envelope flat on the table. He slowly cuts it in half. He makes sure that the scissors don't cut through the lady, but pass over the top of her.

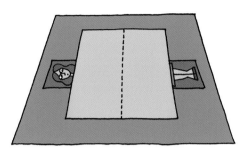

FRONT

10 The magician slowly pulls the lady back through the envelope and holds her up to show that she has not been cut in half.

11 He finishes by holding up the two halves of the cut envelope, then crumpling them up and throwing them away before anyone can see the slits.

WHERE'S THE ORANGE?

ILLUSION

The magician shows a paper carrier bag to the spectators, then fills it with coins, a pen, a notebook and an orange. He decides to eat the orange—but it has turned into a lemon!

1 Prior to the trick, the magician finds a paper carrier bag. He makes sure that the spectators will be no closer than several paces when he does the trick.

2 He cuts a large orange in two and carefully scoops out the flesh.

3 He puts a lemon inside one orange half and carefully reassembles the orange.

4 He places the hollowed-out orange in a bowl containing a couple of other oranges. He should try to avoid revealing the seam where the orange was cut.

5 To perform the trick, the magician sits behind a table with the folded bag, a pencil, a pen, a small notebook, and the bowl of oranges in front of him.

6 He opens the bag and shows it to the spectators. It's important that the spectators see the bag is empty. To make sure they look inside, the magician says, "This sort of flat-bottomed bag holds my stuff really well."

7 He places the bag upright on the table. Then he puts the things in the bag, saying, "Right, I'll need a pencil, maybe a pen, and this notebook."

8 The magician says: "I might get hungry. I'll take an orange." He puts the hollowed-out orange from the fruit bowl into the bag. Then he says, "Mmm ... that orange looked tasty. Maybe I'll have it now."

9 He reaches inside the bag, flips the orange open, and pulls out the lemon.

10 He holds up the lemon and says, "Wait a minute—wasn't that an orange a few seconds ago?!"

ELASTIC BAND UP THE NOSE

1 Prior to the trick, the magician arranges some props—pieces of fruit, a tennis ball, some string, even things he won't be using—on the table.

ILLUSION

The magician paces around a table full of props, secretly fingering an elastic band. He absent-mindedly holds the band near his nose and gives a sniff. The band seems to disappear up his nostril!

2 He loops an elastic band around his right wrist.

3 While walking slowly around the table, the magician stops now and then to pick up some of the props. As he holds a prop, he says "I wonder what that's for," or, "That looks interesting." Then he puts it down and continues.

4 As he continues to walk around the table he chooses a moment when his back is to the audience, then he pulls on the elastic band with his left hand and pinches it between his right thumb and index finger.

5 The magician is now holding an elastic loop about half as long as his little finger.

6 He faces the spectators again. He holds the loop up and says,"What's this? An elastic band. Hmm. Don't need that right now."

7 With a quick motion he puts the band up to his nose and lets go. He makes a loud sniff as he does this, so that the audience won't hear the band snapping back.

8 The spectators think he has sniffed the elastic band into his nostril!

FURTHER READING

Barnhart, Norm. *Amazing Magic Tricks.* Mankato, MN: Capstone Press, 2009.

Cassidy, John and Michael Stroud. *Klutz Book of Magic.* Palo Alto, CA: Klutz Press, 2006.

Charney, Steve. *Cool Card Tricks.* Easy Magic Tricks. Mankato, MN: Capstone Press, 2010.

Klingel, Cynthia and Robert B. Noyed. *Card Tricks.* Games Around the World. Mankato, MN: Compass Point Books, 2002.

Longe, Bob. *The Little Giant Book of Card Tricks.* New York: Sterling Publishers Inc, 2000.

WEBSITES

For web resources related to the subject of this book, go to: www.windmillbooks.com/weblinks and select this book's title.

GLOSSARY

absent-mindedly (AB-sunt MYN-duhd-lee) In a forgetful or distracted way.

index finger (IN-deks FIN-gur) The finger next to the thumb.

reassemble (rih-uh-SEM-buhl) To put back together again.

sleight of hand (SLYT UV HAND) Moving your hands in a sneaky way to confuse the audience.

spectator (SPEK-tay-tur) A person who sees or watches something.

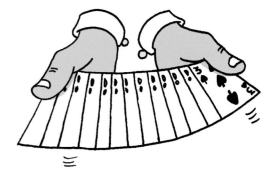

INDEX

B
balls 8, 9, 10, 17, 18, 19
bowls 26, 27, 28

E
elastic band 29, 30, 31
envelopes 22, 23, 24, 25

G
glasses 20, 21

H
hairs 11, 13

O
oranges 26, 27

S
spoons 6, 7
straws 15, 16

W
wands 11, 12, 13, 17, 18, 19
water 20, 21